LEARNING WITH LE
For six- to seven-year-ol

Boy and the Burglar

Story by Irene Yates
Activities by David Bell, Geoff Leyland,
Mick Seller and Irene Yates

Illustrations by Pauline Little

People who live in Cherry Walk

Mum — Dad — Steven — Chris — Harry — Mum — Dad — Beverley
Baby — Jenny — Mark — Kerry — Charley — Wesley — Rose
Pusscuss
Boy

For Mal

It was evening in Cherry Walk.
Outside it was quiet and still.

It was almost bed time.

But there was no settling down
in Cherry Walk.

What time do you think it is in the picture?

How can you tell that it is night time?

What time of year do you think it is?

At number 6 Dad was reading Mark a story.

Mark missed his mum.
'When's she coming home?' he asked.

'It's been a long two weeks,
hasn't it Mark?' smiled Dad.
'But she'll be back from summer school
next weekend.'

How many days are there in two weeks?

On which day do you think Mum might come back?
What do you usually do on that day of the week?

Try saying all the days of the week in the correct order.

Kerry jumped up to answer the phone.

'It's Mum phoning to say goodnight,' she called. 'I'll tell her Mark's playing up.'

'Don't you dare!' screeched Mark.

You can make your own telephone.
You'll need two plastic pots
or cans and a piece of string.

Make a hole in the bottom of each pot.
Pass the string through each one and
tie a knot at both ends.

Make the string taut. Hold one pot
to your ear and ask a friend to talk
into the other one.

What can you hear?
As you're talking, touch the string.
What can you feel?

At number 12 Charley and Wesley were tucking into their supper.

They were going to watch TV for a bit before they went to bed.

But Rose wasn't allowed to.

What's happening in the picture?

Do you watch TV before you go to bed? Make a list of six of your favourite programmes, and give each of them a mark out of ten.

What other things do you like to do in the evening?

Rose stamped around. 'Don't want to go to bed!' she shouted. 'Not fair! Not fair! Not fair! Want to watch the telly!'

'You're not big enough yet!' said Wesley, full of importance.

Charley grinned. 'Little girls need lots of sleep.'

Charley and Wesley's programme starts at 8.35. It lasts for half an hour.
What time will it finish?

Look up today's television programmes. What programmes do you want to watch? Write down the time each of them starts and finishes. Now work out how long you will spend watching TV today.

Beverley was putting on her face.

Rose thought it looked very nice. 'Where are you going?'

'Out, with my friends,' said Beverley. 'When you're as big as me you'll be able to go out too. But right now it's beddybyes for Roses!'

What does 'putting on her face' mean?

Can you think of other funny phrases your mum or dad say to you? Do they say any of these?

'Keep your eyes peeled.'
'You are a pickle!'
'Keep your hair on!'
'Get your skates on.'

Draw pictures of what these phrases really mean.

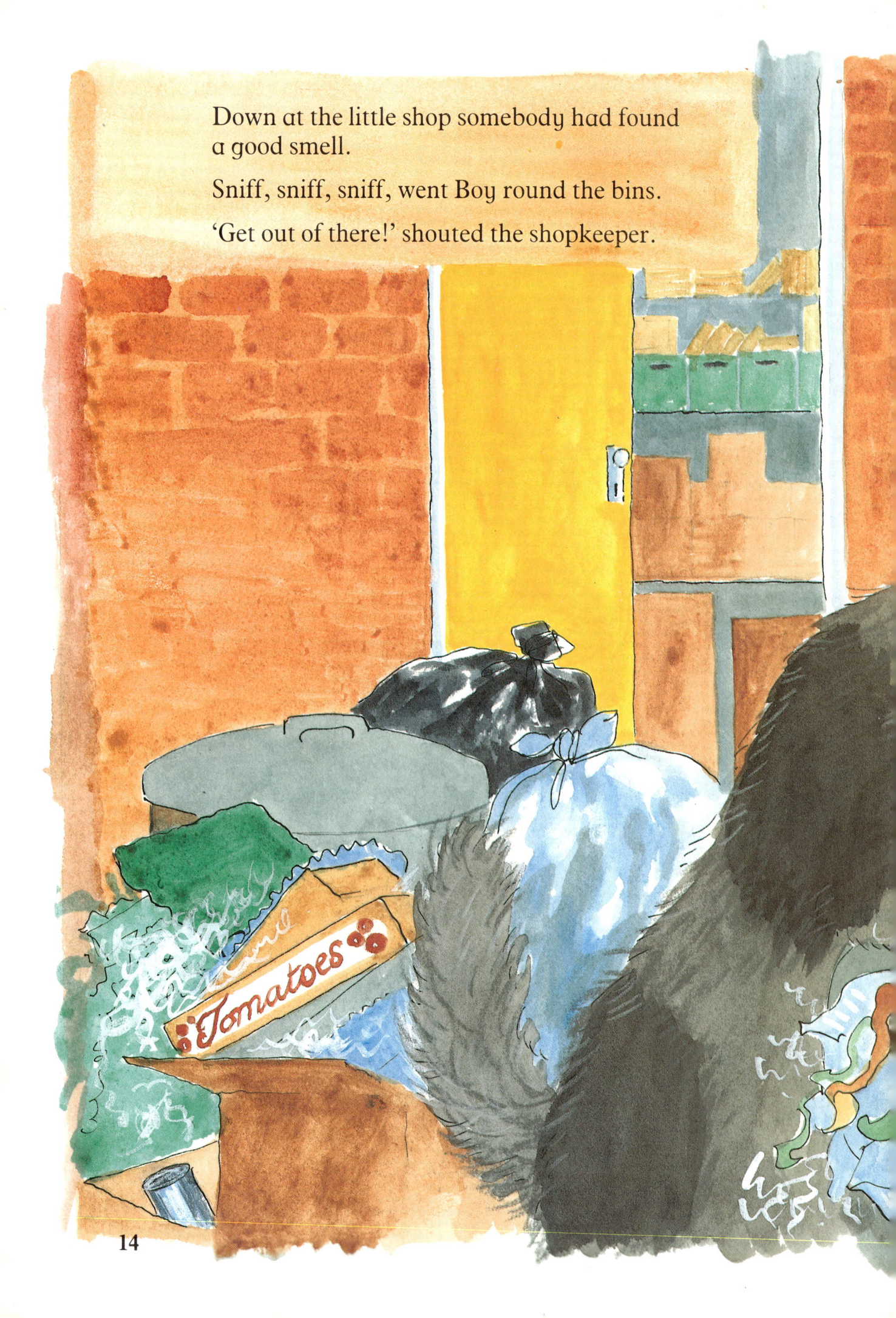

Down at the little shop somebody had found a good smell.

Sniff, sniff, sniff, went Boy round the bins.

'Get out of there!' shouted the shopkeeper.

Talk about what's happening in the picture.
What do you think Boy can smell?

What are your favourite smells?
You could make up a poem, starting
each line with

'I like the smell of ....

See if you can make up ten lines.

She chased Boy out through the gate, but there were so many empty boxes and cartons she didn't see the dog sneak back in.

The shopkeeper locked the back door. 'Another day over,' she sighed, as she climbed the stairs to the flat where she lived.

What can you see behind the door?
What can you see on top of the box?
Where is Boy?
Why can't the shopkeeper see him?

Where is the shopkeeper's flat?

What do you think the shopkeeper is going to do when she gets up the stairs?
Look at what she's carrying.

There were so many interesting smells in the stockroom.
And so much to eat!
There were boxes of biscuits piled up high.
There were cakes. There were Doggie-Chocs.
Boy had a birthday.

What shapes do you recognise?

Can you see any cylinders?
What might be kept in them?
What cylinders can you find in
your house?

How many cuboid shapes can you
see in the picture?
Collect together some cuboid
shaped items in your home.
What is the largest one
you can find?

Then he came upon a nice, snug corner
to curl up in.
He was soon fast asleep, dreaming of marrow-bones
and Doggie-Chocs.

Something made Boy wake up with a start.
What could it be?
He began to growl, very, very quietly.

What was the first thing that happened to Boy in the story?

What happened next?

Can you remember what he had to eat in the stockroom?

What do you think will happen next in the story?

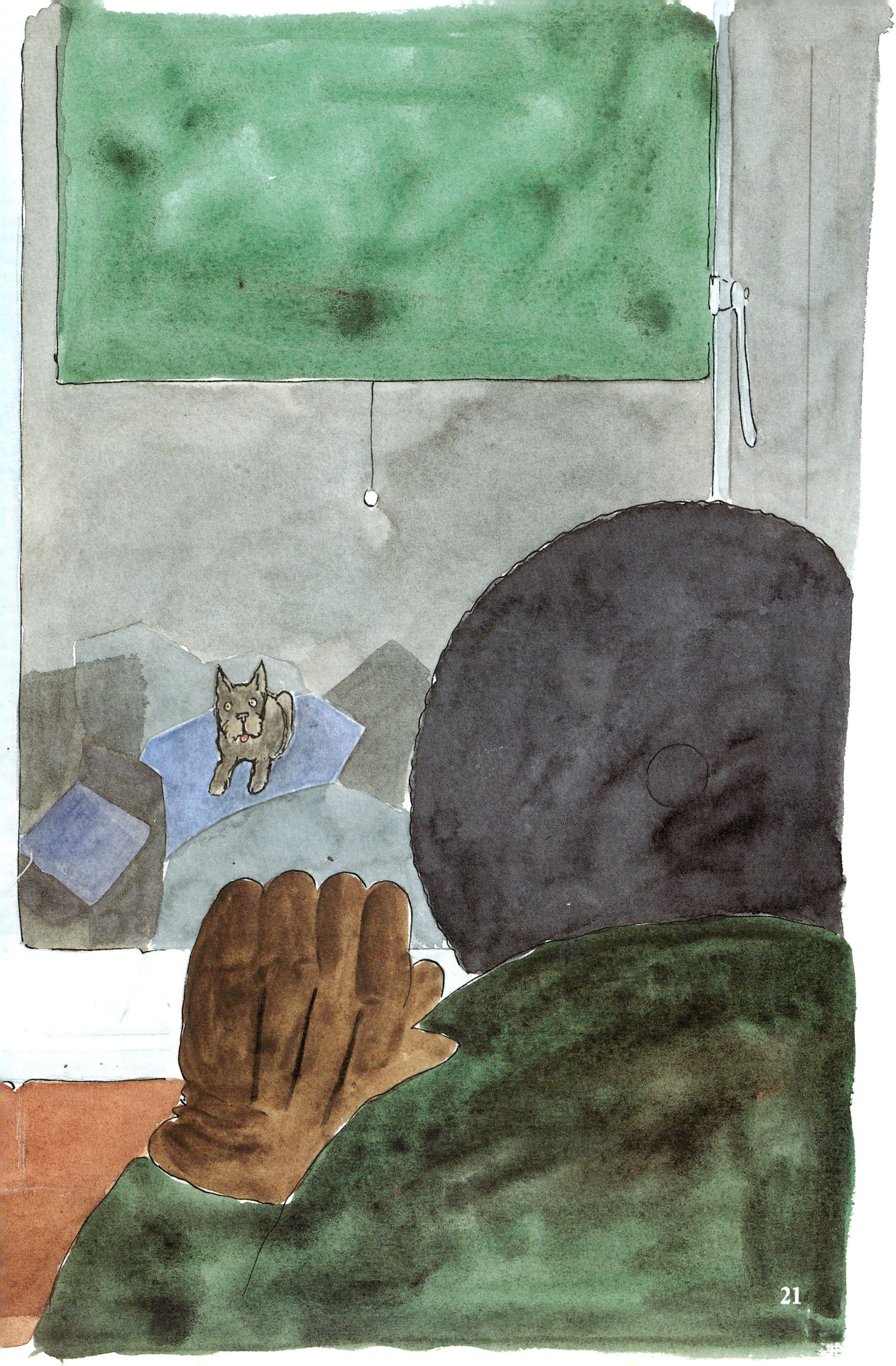

The burglar didn't see Boy until it was much too late.
Up leapt the dog. 'Woof!' he went as loud as he could. 'Woof! Woof! Woof!'

Why do you think the man has a torch?
What do Boy's eyes look like in the light of the torch?

Try holding a piece of card over the end of a torch.
What happens to the beam of light?
Slowly slide the card away.
What happens now?

Make some different shaped holes in some card or paper.

Hold these over the end of the torch.
Shine the beam of light on a wall.
Now move closer to the wall.
What do you notice?

The burglar was in such a hurry to escape from the big fierce dog that he left his shoe behind.

THIS WEEK'S SPECIAL OFFERS!
10p off each of these items
Mini notepads 40p now
Pencils 20p now
Rubbers 35p now

Look at the poster showing the special offers.
Work out the new prices.

You could set up a shop at home using tins and packets.
You could sell all of them at 10p off the normal price.
Write out a list of special prices on a large piece of paper.
Now you are ready for your customers!

'Now then!' called the shopkeeper. 'What's going on? What's all this noise about?'

First she saw Boy.
Then she saw the shoe.
Then she saw the open window.

Look at the shoe the burglar left behind.
Is it much bigger than your shoes?
What size do you take?

What sizes do other people in your family take?

You could find some large pieces of paper and draw round the feet of everyone in your family.
Who has the biggest feet?
Who has the smallest feet?

'It's a good job you did sneak in!'
said the shopkeeper, patting Boy on the head.
'Now we'd better call the police.'

This is the kind of clue a policeman may look for. You could make a shoeprint like this. Try it in some wet sand or soil.

Collect different shoes and boots.
Take turns in making prints with them.

Play this 'Guess the print' game.
Make a print with one of the shoes.
Can Mum or Dad guess which shoe you used?
Perhaps you could use only the heel or sole of a shoe to make it harder!

'Don't worry,' said the policeman.
'We'll soon catch the burglar.'

The shopkeeper patted Boy on the head.
'Good dog!'

Cherry Walk settled down for the night at last.

How do you think the policeman will catch the burglar?

How do you think the shopkeeper feels now? Where do you think Boy is going to spend the night?

How many people would you need if you were going to act out this story?
Where in the story would you start the acting?
Get together with some friends.
Try acting out the story without using any words.

Activity notes

Pages 2–3 Children develop a sense of time by associating particular times with events in their day. Your child will probably know, for example, the times when they usually get up, go to school, have lunch, arrive home, have tea, go to bed. You could make a 'clock diary' together, listing the events of the day in one column, the times they happen in another.

Pages 4–5 Reciting the names of the days of the week is something that young children soon learn to do. By talking about family plans you can help your child associate different days with particular events. Making a colourful wall calendar for the week or fortnight can be useful too. Include all the family activities – it will be a reminder to everyone!

Pages 6–7 In this activity your child is investigating the connection between sound and vibration. If they touch the string very lightly as they talk, they will be able to feel it vibrating.

Pages 8–9 Encourage your child to talk about and give reasons for choosing particular TV programmes. This will develop logical thinking and will help them to take a fuller part in classroom discussions.

Pages 10–11 This activity is about handling data. Obtaining information from television guides, timetables and other public notices is an important everyday maths skill. Working out the difference between two times is quite complex, so your child may need some help.

Pages 12–13 Children love playing with funny words or expressions. You could help your child realise that many of the jokes they so much enjoy involve playing with words!

Pages 14–15 Writing poems helps children to use more descriptive vocabulary and to choose words with care. The senses involve personal experience and are a good starting point for writing poems.

Pages 16–17 Using positional words such as 'behind', 'on top of', and 'under', is important in maths as well as in English. You could take it in turns to hide an object in the room. Give clues as to how to find it, like 'it's under a chair', 'it's behind a book'.

Pages 18–19 Children often confuse two- and three-dimensional shapes, eg they call a cylinder a circle, or a cube a square. Help them to see that a two-dimensional shape has only one face and that a three-dimensional shape has a number of faces.

Pages 20–21 Remembering the sequence of events helps to develop an awareness of order and pattern, and is therefore a maths skill as well as a language one. Sometimes asking questions about your child's day at school will help them put events in order, eg 'Did you do that before playtime?', 'What did you do just after assembly?'

Pages 22–23 Here your child is finding out what happens to a beam of light in different circumstances. They may want to carry out further investigations of their own.

Pages 24–25 Playing shopping games can provide good practice in simple addition and subtraction. Start with prices in small amounts of money and just take 1p or 2p off. As children's confidence increases, they will be able to deal with larger amounts.

Pages 26–27 Children are fascinated by their own personal statistics, such as their shoe size, height, weight. Making comparisons between themselves and other members of the family is a useful early measuring activity. Later your child can be expected to handle standard units of measurement.

Pages 28–29 Looking for similarities and differences and noticing patterns are all part of careful observation. Playing the shoeprint game will encourage your child to look for patterns in other objects.

Pages 30–31 Acting out the story involves remembering who said or did what, getting the events in the right order, retelling it in different words. Children who decide to mime the story will probably need some help from you.

About the authors and advisers

Irene Yates is a writer and teacher in charge of language development at Lakey Lane School in Birmingham.

David Bell is Assistant Director of Education (Forward Planning) for Newcastle upon Tyne City Council, a former primary head and maths specialist.

Geoff Leyland is Deputy Head of Deer Park Primary School in Derbyshire and a former science and technology advisory teacher.

Mick Seller is Deputy Head of Asterdale Primary School in Derbyshire and a former science and technology advisory teacher.

Elizabeth Bassant is a language advisory teacher in Haringey, London. **Peter Ovens** is Principal Lecturer for Curriculum and Professional Development at Nottingham Polytechnic and a science specialist. **Peter Patilla** is a maths consultant, author and Senior Lecturer in Mathematics Education at Sheffield Polytechnic.

Margaret Williams is an advisory teacher for maths in Newton Abbot, Devon.